A
DIVINE
PAUSE

FINDING YOUR PATH TO HIS PRESENCE

S. DEE CLARK-RILEY

Copyright © 2021 S. Dee Clark-Riley

Unless otherwise indicated, all Scripture quotations are taken from the Holy Bible, New Living Translation, copyright © 1996, 2004, 2015 by Tyndale House Foundation. Used by permission of Tyndale House Publishers, Inc., Carol Stream, Illinois 60188. All rights reserved. "Scripture quotations are from the ESV® Bible (The Holy Bible, English Standard Version®), copyright © 2001 by Crossway, a publishing ministry of Good News Publishers. Used by permission. All rights reserved." Scripture quotations from The Authorized (King James) Version. Rights in the Authorized Version in the United Kingdom are vested in the Crown. Reproduced by permission of the Crown's patentee, Cambridge University Press

All rights reserved. No part of this document may be reproduced or transmitted in any form or by any means, electronic, mechanical, photocopying, recording, or otherwise, without prior written permission of the author.

A DIVINE PAUSE
Finding Your Path To His Presence

S. Dee Clark-Riley
dee3271@gmail.com

ISBN 978-1-949826-29-6
Printed in the USA.
All rights reserved

Published by: EAGLES GLOBAL BOOKS | Frisco, Texas
In conjunction with the 2021 Eagles Authors Course
Cover & interior designed by DestinedToPublish.com

DEDICATION

This book is dedicated to the women of my breast cancer support group at Scott AFB and to breast cancer survivors everywhere. Thank you. -"Girl, you got this!"

A Divine Pause

ACKNOWLEDGEMENTS

First, I must acknowledge Father God for surrounding me with a great support team:

Eagle Nation- Y'all showed up and showed out as always! I love you.

JUDAH Dance Ministry- Thank you. We are family for real!

My Mary Kay family (too many to name)- Thank you for the countless cards, notes, gifts, and check-ins. *Pink Changing Lives* forever!

My bestie's in every situation Twanna Cunningham and Yaneka Willis- Thank you for holding my hand, coordinating care and meals, and just loving on me and my family. I am eternally grateful.

A Divine Pause

Last but certainly not least, my mom, Sharon Clark-Napolitano- Thank you for flying in for every treatment and surgery during the pandemic to take care of me. You masked up and made it happen, just for me. I love you Mama, to infinity and beyond.

FOREWORD

From the first time I met Dee, I noticed that she exuded strength and confidence in who she was as a person and a child of God. I used to wonder, "How does one come to have that level of confidence and how do I get there?". Upon our meeting, I was still in the process of finding myself in life as well as in Christ. Dee has always been my go-to person when I am experiencing stress and chaos in my life. She always has a timely word that pulls me off the edge of the cliff. Dee has always been a person that seeks God fiercely and I have always admired this quality of hers.

Dee is the person that you come to you when you have a problem because she always has a word from God. She never shows frustration or stress no matter how frustrating or stressful the situation is. I love that she has chosen to share with the world how she seeks God so fiercely. The world will get to experience what I experience every time we have a conversation.

We can all relate to how tumultuous and chaotic 2020 was. One problem was that not many were strategic about navigating it. What started off as a year of victory quickly became a year of confusion and uncertainty. Many struggled because they lacked what we call self-care. No one was used to being locked down without any control or any idea of what to expect next. For those who knew to seek God, it sometimes proved difficult to keep up. We were all lost, and some continue to be lost, trying to find their way back to normal. Although we are beginning to open back up as a world, nothing is what it was. This book helps us learn how to navigate any chaotic situations we may face in the future.

I love how Dee gets straight to the point. When you are facing turmoil within your life, the last thing you want is to be toyed with regarding how to achieve victory. She tells you about just that; while giving you fact-based solutions that work and letting you know what God says about you. I love how she wasn't afraid to talk about her journey and what she continues to experience as a result. Transparency is key when helping the next person understand or know that they too can be victorious in the midst of a chaotic situation. I'm always looking for ways in which I can strengthen my relationship with God, and this book has helped open my eyes to ways in which I need to or can incorporate the Word of God in my daily life. One Scripture that I find myself speaking daily in my morning devotional is Psalm 19:14, *"May these words of my mouth and this meditation of my heart be pleasing/acceptable in your sight Lord".*

This book covers many benefits of meditation I incorporate into the therapeutic process with my clients. It's particularly important that we all take some time to meditate daily. Doing so brings balance in stressful situations. Meditation in and of itself has healing properties when implemented on a daily basis. It's extremely important to know your body and how it reacts to stress. Meditation helps with this. I am a firm believer in meditation, but I also understand that it is a learned behavior. If you don't take the time to learn how to implement it in your life you will find yourself in a constant cycle of frustration and stress. I pray that this book blesses you as it has blessed me. I know that I will be intentional about taking a DIVINE PAUSE and seeking God daily.

A Divine Pause

TABLE OF CONTENTS

How to Use this Book xi

Introduction xiii

Chapter 1: Meditation is? 1

Chapter 2: Meditation and the Scriptures 7

Chapter 3: The Benefits of Meditation 13

Chapter 4: Pathways to His Presence 18

Chapter 5: Time with Daddy God 22

Conclusion 75

Meditation Resources 77

References and Cited Works 79

A Divine Pause

HOW TO USE THIS BOOK

At the beginning of the book, I give a little background information on meditation from Eastern and Western perspectives. Then I discuss meditation from a biblical standpoint, making a connection between it and intimacy with Christ. Along with the spiritual benefits of meditation, I explain its physical and emotional/mental benefits. Finally, I present meditation tips, techniques, and strategies that anyone can learn. I wrote this book while going through breast cancer treatment. Though I was a novice in the practice, it was highly instrumental in my healing and sanity.

This book is designed to be an interactive experience. Keep a tandem document handy to record anything from your exercises. Resist the urge to rush through the reading. But, if you do, just go back and read again, no judgement. The goal is to help you discover what meditation looks like for you in order to abide in HIS Presence.

A Divine Pause

INTRODUCTION

Much like many of you, I had 2020 all planned out. It was the year of my "Release". My calendar was filled with ministry assignments and vacation plans. It was the year when I would retire from the military after 26 years of service. I was excited for what laid ahead. I was stepping all the way into my "Calling" from the Lord unapologetically.

March 2020: I returned home from a speaking engagement in Dallas to find out that we were experiencing a pandemic. Because I'd been preparing for the event, I hadn't watched the news or any TV for that matter. I knew what was happening in the nursing homes in Washington State but that was the extent of it. I couldn't believe what was happening. I couldn't believe there were no paper towels or toilet paper anywhere in my city. What was happening?

A Divine Pause

My work trip at the end of the month was cancelled. This had become the norm where the rest of my itinerary was concerned. Military work had become exhausting. As Command Staff, we were responsible for leading, guiding, and directing the Chaplain Corp during the pandemic. This was a new battlefield. While people were dying, my team couldn't assist with the "last rites" because they didn't have personal protective equipment (PPE). What about church and worship services for the troops and the community? Those were just a few of the myriad of issues we had to figure out in a COVID-19 environment. I worked long hours and took a lot of the stress home because I wanted to help but didn't know how. I wanted solutions.

We had daily prayer at work. Right there in the office, we prayed. Our calls with the Pentagon began with prayer. We needed to acknowledge that something bigger than ourselves was in control. As soon as one victory manifested, another challenge came. Like many others, we were also dealing with COVID-19 challenges. Our families were getting sick and dying too. It was a lot.

April 2020: Work had become overwhelming. When I checked in with our members from other bases, I learned that they were stressed to capacity. Many of them were working from home and trying to take care of their kids because schools were closed. Others were doing double or triple duty because a co-worker or family member had tested positive and would be out for 7-14 days.

Introduction

Amid all of this, I had 2 small businesses that were failing due to the shutdown. The stress was unbearable and I needed a break. I took a week of leave to calm my spirit and take care of me. During my time off I found a lump in my left breast. With COVID-19 now running rampant, I didn't want to go see a doctor. Another week went before I called to make an appointment. My primary care provider recommended that I get a mammogram as soon as possible. I had one scheduled for the following week. The lump I felt was confirmed to be "suspicious" and I ended up needing a biopsy. A week later, on May 12th to be exact, the lump was indeed diagnosed as breast cancer. Cancer in the midst of COVID! Cancer before I could retire!

Nothing was going as planned. I had to find a way to maintain my sanity. I had to find a way to increase my faith. I had to find a way to lead in the midst of a crisis. I had to find peace in the chaos.

Praying helped temporarily, but what I was experiencing was new. I needed a new experience with God. I had to go deeper or I would die.

A Divine Pause

CHAPTER 1
MEDITATION IS?

med·i·tate /ˈmedəˌtāt/ verb

1. think deeply or focus one's mind for a period of time, in silence or with the aid of chanting, for religious or spiritual purposes or as a method of relaxation.
2. think deeply or carefully about (something).
3. plan mentally; consider.

As you can see from the definitions above, to meditate is not a bad thing. We do it often when planning a meeting for work, studying for a test or crafting the perfect speech or sermon. Meditation is simply the process of thinking deeply or carefully about something.

According to my research, experts agree that the practice of meditation pre-dates the birth of modern civilization. I think it gets a bad rap in the Christian community for a few reasons.

First, it's thought of as psychological manipulation. Second, its ancient practices in the Chinese Taoist and Buddhist traditions. The Buddha, who lived and taught in Southeast Asia about 2,600 years ago, founded the practice of sitting in mindful awareness and breathing one's way to peace. According to Buddhism, meditative concentration combined with ethical conduct and the wisdom of seeing things as they truly are result in an awakening or enlightenment.

Swami Vivekanda & Paramahansa Yoganda introduced and popularized meditation and yoga in the West in the early 20th century. Many traveled to the East to train in Asian countries to bring their knowledge of mindfulness back home and share it.

Buddhist meditation usually involves mantras which edify the gods of either Buddhism or Hinduism. Meditating on and chanting a word or phrase praising or seeking a false god is contradictory to the principles of Christianity. This brings me to yoga. I was on a 6-month military tour in Colorado Springs, Colorado and wanted something different to do to break up the monotony of my fitness routine. I found a Groupon for 10 sessions of Hot Yoga. I really didn't know what that would entail but the price was right, and it was across the street from my downtown apartment. I paid for the Groupon and signed up for my sessions. Now, before the purchase, I knew that some Yoga practices such as chants and mantras that edify other gods, were against my beliefs. So, I made up my mind that whenever they said something I did not understand or agree with, I would say, "The joy of the Lord is

Meditation is?

my strength," or "You are the Alpha and the Omega King Jesus," or any other phrase that came to mind that would edify my GOD. I arrived early for my first session because I was excited. When I entered the studio there was a pleasant vibe to the place. The waiting area was chill, and members of the staff were very welcoming. I could tell that the other ladies waiting with me were regulars. They had their own thick mats and cute yoga clothes on. Eventually, it was time to go in for our session. The three other ladies took their usual spots and the instructor led me to a spot on the end. About 6 feet directly in front of me was the Buddha. I immediately starting sweating and couldn't tell if it was from my view or the heat in the studio; it was hot yoga.

I was uncomfortable. I tried to find other interesting things to look at in the room. I felt like the Buddha was watching me. After a few awkward poses, I decided to look the statue in the eye. It was totally irrational for me to be fearful. As I turned my gaze to face the statue, I noticed that my car's trunk was open through the big picture window behind it. Downtown C-Springs was not the best neighborhood, so I politely excused myself to close the trunk. When I returned, I took my assigned spot and continued the workout, praying and quoting Scripture with every move. During the cool down (Lol! Hot yoga) I noticed my trunk was open again. Once more, I politely excused myself and went to take care of it. When I returned, they were finishing up with a mantra and class was dismissed. As you can tell, this was not a relaxing experience. It was certainly no escape from my busy day. I believe Holy Spirit was leading me out of that class, and I refused to hear it. I never had a problem with the trunk spontaneously opening after that.

MINDFULNESS

> mind·ful·ness /ˈmīn(d)f(ə)lnəs/ noun
> 1. the quality or state of being conscious or aware of something.
> 2. a mental state achieved by focusing one's awareness on the present moment, while calmly acknowledging and accepting one's feelings, thoughts, and bodily sensations, used as a therapeutic technique.

Generally speaking, mindfulness is a technique of deliberately focusing your attention on the present. You don't let yourself get distracted by the other thoughts that are constantly running through your head; you clear the noise from your mind.

Mindfulness is all about being present and aware of our surroundings. This allows us to be fully present. The decrease in anxiety comes from the free of judgement and awareness of thoughts and feelings aspects of mindfulness. When one no longer judges their own thoughts or desires, and does not get caught up in their feelings, they feel safer and calmer. Therefore, they become less anxious.

Mindfulness and mediation are often used and practiced synonymously. In the secular sense, the focus is horizontal.

Your attention is on you and stays on you. The secular practice is about detaching yourself and merging with the cosmic mind. There is no God to attach to or hear from. Scripture, however, teaches us to have the mind of Christ and to evaluate everything in the light of our vertical relationship with the Father. We detach to attach to our Holy Father.

Secular meditation and mindfulness can be dangerous. Luke 11:24-26 says the following, *[24] When an impure spirit comes out of a person, if it goes through arid places seeking rest and does not find it. Then it says, 'I will return to the house I left.' [25] When it arrives, it finds the house swept clean and put in order. [26] Then it goes and takes seven other spirits more wicked than itself, and they go in and live there. And the final condition of that person is worse than the first.* As Christians, our practice must include an attachment to the Holy Spirit and getting filled up with God's Word. We can't leave the door open for the enemy to invade and trample on our peace. Mindfulness and meditation should lead us to the inner wholeness that is necessary for us to freely give ourselves to God.

In my virtual breast cancer support group, we had a guest speaker who was an expert in mindfulness. It was interesting. She had us sit up and make sure our feet were flat on the ground. After we engaged in some deep breathing, she asked us to imagine we were trees. It went something like this: "You are tall, strong, and solid. You are old and wise. Bring awareness to your feet and notice them in contact with the ground. They are firmly grounded. Now, imagine roots extending from the bottoms of your feet, pushing downward from the surface, and reaching into the soil. Feel yourself anchored to the ground by your extensive root system." You get the picture. It was quite elaborate, and my mind was wandered throughout the exercise. The experience was definitely horizontal, but I was intrigued enough to want to learn more. It's funny how one's perspective or position regarding something changes when it's a matter of life and death. I needed a new way to find intimacy with God. I needed a DIVINE PAUSE.

CHAPTER 2

MEDITATION AND THE SCRIPTURES

Christians and many faith-based counselors use mindfulness in a Christ-integrated way as a therapy tool. The exercises are rooted in Scripture and focus on connecting with God.

In fact, the Word teaches us to meditate. The following words are translated in Hebrew and Greek (respectively) into our English word for meditate:

> Hagah: muse, growl, moan, utter (Strong's 1897). Found in: Joshua 1:8, Job 27:4, Jeremiah 48:31, as well as various times in Psalms, Proverbs, and Isaiah.

> Suach: muse (Strong's 7742). The Complete Word Study Bible further expands on the use of this word to mean, "a verb meaning to be bowed down; to be downcast. It refers often to the despair of one's soul." Found in: Genesis 24:63.

Meletaō: to care for, practice, study (Strong's 3191). Found in: Acts 4:25, 1 Timothy 4:15.

The first person we see "meditating" in the Bible is Isaac. He is meditating (suach) in a field when the Lord brings his wife (Genesis 24:63). Isaac is the son God promised to Abraham and Sarah. He is too old to be a bachelor, but there he is, waiting on the Lord's provision for a wife. He is in the midst of grieving the death of his mother, meditating and waiting when God brings Rebekah to him. The Scripture says he took Rebekah as his wife, loved her all his days, and was comforted after his mother's death. Isaacs' life of meditation and prayer led to the Lord blessing him with a family. (April Motl. www.christianity.com)

Then there is Joshua. After Moses dies, the Lord gives instructions to Joshua, Moses' aide. One instruction is to meditate on the Book of the Law. *"This Book of the Law shall not depart from your mouth, but you shall meditate [hagah] on it day and night, so that you may be careful to do according to all that is written in it; for then you will make your way prosperous, and then you will have success."* Joshua 1:8. The Psalms echo this admonition; similarly, offering the results of strength, health, and prosperity (Psalms 1:2-3).

So, why don't more Christians mediate? Many Believers are content with hearing from God through a third party or resource. They want the Prophet to prophesy to them, the Pastor to lay hands on them, or they want to receive the Word from a worship

Meditation and the Scriptures

service or conference. These are not the Old Testament days when only the high priest could enter the Holy of Holies. There is no need for a mediator other than Jesus. The middleman is no more. Meditation calls us to enter the Presence of God for ourselves and to hear His voice. Meditation makes us accountable. God is speaking and wants us to hear and obey Him.

Another reason why Christian's don't practice meditation is simply their lack of knowledge. In its basic form, meditation is biblical. Using Scripture as part of one's practice is necessary and helpful; it enables the Believer to concentrate and embed the doctrines, law, and testimony that are vital for their spirituality.

So I wondered, "Who in my circle actually uses meditation regularly?" I surveyed 100 contacts and asked them the following questions:

1. Do you mediate?
2. Why or Why Not?
3. If applicable, how do you meditate?

To my surprise, 40% answered yes to number 1. Those who mediated used the practice to calm down, seek peace, and connect with God. Those who did not meditate gave reasons such as the following, "I used to and need to get back to it", I don't believe in it", "I don't know how" and "I don't have time." I learned from the survey and a few follow-up conversations that almost 100% of my contacts meditated! However, because they associated the word with the Buddhist and Hindu traditions, they chose to call their actions something else. Again, meditation is not taboo; it's biblical.

ACTIVATION-
Here are a few tips to help root the WORD in your heart:

> **1. Start and end your day with the Word.**
>
> If we read the Word in the morning, it's easy for it to slip out of our thoughts over the course of the day. Busy schedules and demands can quickly replace those life-giving verses from our morning devotion. I personally must read and write the Scriptures. This helps me with my memorization.
>
> **2. Do something with the Word.**
>
> Doing something with what we read, helps to keep God's word at the forefront of our thoughts. Essentially, whether you do correlative study with a Bible passage, make crafts with verses, or make a song from a verse, doing something with the words helps you to hold on to them. If you can remember them, then you can meditate on them. There will be more on this in the next chapter.
>
> **3. Talk about God's Word.**
>
> If we talk regularly about God's Word, we will meditate on God's Word. And if we talk and think about God's word, we will be more able to obey God's Word. Moreover, if we obey God's Word, our lives will be better positioned for His blessings!

The rest of this chapter comprises Scriptures for your reference.

David: Psalm 19:14, *May these words of my mouth and this meditation of my heart be pleasing in your sight, Lord, my Rock and my Redeemer.*

Sons of Korah: Psalm 48:9, *Within your temple, O God, we meditate on your unfailing love.*

Asaph: Psalm 77:12, *I will consider all your works and meditate on all your mighty deeds.*

David: Psalm 119:15, *I meditate on your precepts and consider your ways.*

Paul: 1 Timothy 4:15, *Meditate on these things; give yourself entirely to them, that your progress may be evident to all.*

Paul: Philippians 4:8, *Finally, brethren, whatever things are true, whatever things are noble, whatever things are just, whatever things are pure, whatever things are lovely, whatever things are of good report, if there is any virtue and if there is anything praiseworthy—meditate on these things.*

Here are yet more Scriptures:

Paul: Colossians 3:2-4, *Set your minds on things above, not on earthly things. For you died, and your life is now hidden with Christ in God. When Christ, who is your life, appears, then you also will appear with him in glory.*

Paul: Romans 6:6-8, *The mind governed by the flesh is death, but the mind governed by the Spirit is life and peace. The mind governed by the flesh is hostile to God; it does not submit to God's law, nor can it do so. Those who are in the realm of the flesh cannot please God.*

The Old and New Testaments remind us that where we set our thoughts will greatly impact the fruitfulness of our lives. Think on good things and take a DIVINE PAUSE.

CHAPTER 3
THE BENEFITS OF MEDITATION

PHYSICAL HEALTH

Research suggests that meditation can help manage the symptoms of anxiety, asthma, cancer, chronic pain, depression, heart disease, high blood pressure, irritable bowel syndrome, sleep problems, and tension headaches.

I found this to be true for me where sleep, chronic pain, and tension headaches were concerned. Chemotherapy was the main contributor to the pain and headaches. The severe bone pain was the worst I'd ever felt. I had to be helped out of bed and could hardly walk. I felt like I was 90 years old. The drug they gave me to decrease the bone pain made it worse. Even in that state, I was able to meditate and hear God's comforting Word using one of my apps. The app also had bedtime stories that helped me fall asleep. The hydrocodone I was taking helped too.

The Lord knows our bodies because He created them. This is why we experience health benefits when we choose to focus our minds and meditate on Him.

MENTAL/EMOTIONAL HEALTH
The primary reason why people meditate is to reduce stress. This was certainly my #1. I could not eat, sleep, drink, think straight, or stay focused. I was stressed to the max. This was unusual for me. I am normally calm and able to navigate through stressful situations well. That caused me more distress and my body reacted.

Because you are reading this book, I feel it's safe to say you are looking for a way to improve your mental and emotional health too. To me, 2020 was an experience like no other. Social injustice, the pandemic, government foolishness (on both sides), financial hardships, death, and not being able to grieve and memorialize loved one's normally were a lot to deal with. You may have a few more things to add to the list; cancelled and rescheduled life events such as weddings, milestone birthdays and anniversaries, graduations, and vacations. Our mental health is important and we must not take it lightly.

Meditating clears away the information overload that builds up every day and contributes to your stress. The emotional benefits of meditation can include your gaining a new perspective on stressful situations, building skills to manage your stress, increasing your self-awareness, focusing on the present, reducing your negative emotions, increasing your imagination and creativity, and increasing your patience and tolerance.

Meditation sends us into the world with the perspective and balance to handle any situation that arises.

Going through cancer treatment is tough but necessary. My mental and emotional health is challenged daily. Some examples of this are evident in a recent journal entry of mine:

April 2021

I recently completed 30 rounds of radiation treatment. My skin is charred. I am tired. The pain is sometimes unbearable. I didn't know how I was going to get through it. The thought of going in day after day was defeating. But I did it. Now that it's over I feel lost. I don't have another oncology appointment until May. Is the cancer gone? I know I am healed. The Lord confirmed it a few weeks ago at 5:18 AM, but...I want some lab report to say so. That is so contradictory to what we say as Christians, "Who's report are you going to believe?" and our response, " I believe the Lord's report!". This is another reason I meditate. If I don't stay in God's face, I get sidetracked and confused about who is really in control.

I have hot flashes regularly now. Chemotherapy kicked me into menopause, and it sucks. To make matters worse, the medication I have to take causes severe hot flashes and mood swings. I am torn at this point as to whether to continue with the Tamoxifen or quit taking it. If I'm healed, why am I taking it in the first place? Help me Jesus. This is why I meditate. I need clarity for this walk. The truth in God's Word gives light to the path. I know that's a Scripture somewhere.

So I'm writing this book about meditation and how it helped me during cancer treatments. But NOW, I can't seem to force myself to continue meditating. Why? I still need peace. I still need time with God. Perhaps meditation needs to take a different form.

As you can see, the battle in my mind is real. I can feel it when I'm getting anxious. It's an uneasy feeling. It's that foreboding spirit that does not want to let me relax and rest in God. It's at these times that I must stop and meditate. I take a few deep, cleansing breaths and begin to quote Scriptures or my personal affirmations. I need a DIVINE PAUSE.

SPIRITUAL HEALTH

"True contemplation is not a psychological trick but a theological grace"-Thomas Merton

There are spiritual benefits to meditation.

One is peace. My phrase for 2021 is "Joy and Peace." In all situations, I will find the path to joy and peace. Our spirits find peace when we meditate on the works of God. For example, meditating on the fact that God is for you and not against you will remind your spirit that there is peace in Him. Throughout the Psalms we see Davids' example of directing his thoughts to Scripture and to his past experiences with God when life becomes difficult.

Spiritually speaking, meditating on God allows us to grow in intimacy with Him. The more time we spend thinking about and dwelling on His character, the closer our spirits are to Him. In this way, we find spiritual intimacy with our Father and Creator.

When we meditate on God's trustworthiness, we find that our spirit trust in Him more. This goes for all the characteristics of God. When we meditate on who He is, our spirits connect with Him. The Creator of all things desires to fellowship with us.

Meditation is an act of devotion to our Lord. It's the choice to take a bold step forward and move away from the crowd. This connection with the Father gives way to our hearing the will of God. When you need clarity, direction, strength, courage, peace, joy, love, help, healing, and hope, take a DIVINE PAUSE and seek HIM.

CHAPTER 4

PATHWAYS TO HIS PRESENCE

"The mind governed by the flesh is death, but the mind governed by the Spirit is life and peace. The mind governed by the flesh is hostile to God; it does not submit to God's law, nor can it do so. Those who are in the realm of the flesh cannot please God." (Romans 6:6-8)

GUIDED MEDITATION

- A narrator or "guide" talks you through the meditation experience

- Wikipedia: Guided meditation describes a form of meditation which utilizes a number of different techniques to achieve or enhance the meditative state. It may simply be meditation done under the guidance of a trained practitioner or teacher, or it may be through the use of imagery, music, and other techniques.

Sometimes I don't know what to do or say; I just know I feel anxious. *"Be anxious for nothing..." Philippians 4:6-7.* In these instances, I often use one of my apps to help quiet my mind. The narrator guides me through a few exercises to help calm my spirit and remind me HE is truly in control.

If you have trouble sleeping or settling down for the night, a guided meditative bedtime story works great! Not only does it relax you, but you also fall asleep with God's WORD in your heart. It's so peaceful! Guided meditation is excellent for the novice or expert.

CONTEMPLATIVE PRAYER

The Eastern Orthodox Church has a three-level hierarchy of prayer. The first level of prayer is vocal prayer, the second level is meditation (also called inward prayer or discursive prayer), and the third level is contemplative prayer, in which a much closer relationship with God is cultivated.

Contemplative prayer is thought to be the highest form of prayer which aims to achieve a close spiritual union with God. Both Eastern and Western Christian teachings have emphasized the use of meditative prayers as an element of increasing one's knowledge of Christ.

James W. Goll explains, "Contemplative prayer immerses us into the silence of God and helps us let go of control of our own life that leans on the props of this world for fulfillment.

It is communion with God that increases our awareness of His presence. As we become more aware of His presence, we are more willing to submit to the Holy Spirit's cleansing work of purification bringing us to a place of surrender"(godencounter.com).

SOAKING PRAYER

Soaking prayer is time set aside for dedication to the Lord and to declare to Him that He is your *one thing*. It is a promise to God that this time is set aside for no other purpose than to commune with Him. Soaking prayer is an invitation to the Father declaring, "God, do what you want to in me. Here I am. I am yours, and you are mine."

"Soaking" is a more familiar term for meditation in the African American community. It's usually done with music and narrated prayers.

As we rest expectantly in prayer, the Holy Spirit will often hover over us to reveal more of God's love or to renew and repair areas of brokenness in our lives. As the Believer soaks in God's presence, the Lord takes control and begins to draw their attention to God's will in their lives. This could occur through a revelation of Scripture, or through impressions or pictures that God shows them.

John Arnott compares soaking prayer to the process of making pickles. "I found a classical Greek word study on the words 'bapto', meaning 'to dip', and 'baptidzo', meaning to immerse. ... The recipe called for the raw fruit to be dipped in boiling water to blanch or sterilize the cucumber, using the word 'bapto', which means, 'to dip in and out quickly'. Then it called for the cucumber to be immersed, using the word 'baptidzo', and soaked in the brine and the pickling solution for several weeks. What happens during this soaking time is that the marinade or the pickling solution soaks deep into the flesh of the cucumber until it takes on the flavor of the pickling solution so that it no longer tastes like a raw cucumber."

"This is what we mean by soaking," Arnott explains. "May you be so marinated in the presence of the Holy Spirit, soaking in the River of God, that you no longer 'taste' like your old, raw nature, but you have taken on the flavor of the Holy Spirit. 'Pickle us Lord, in the marinade of the Holy Spirit. Soak us in your wonderful presence until we become more and more like you"(Johnandcarol.org; soaking in the spirit).

CHAPTER 5

TIME WITH DADDY GOD

"I go through life as a transient on his way to eternity, made in the image of God but with that image debased, needing to be taught how to meditate, to worship, to think."-Donald Coggan

It's almost impossible to learn how to meditate from a book. You just have to do it. Like anything, it takes practice to master it. In fact, the enemy will throw things into your path to discourage you from continuing. It's definitely a learned discipline. You may feel like your meditations have little meaning, but I guarantee there is progression in spiritual life. Don't give up. Pray for grace and the desire to meditate and God will anoint you for it.

Here's my prayer for you:

Father you are the Alpha and Omega, the Beginning and the End, The Creator of the universe. You know ALL things. You have divinely called your child to take a divine pause. Father, I ask that you cover them as they embark on their mediation journey. You know why it's needed so I ask you to grace them to do it. I ask that you give them a desire and a thirst for meditation in whatever form you call them to practice. Let their time with you be fulfilling. Hear their prayers and pleas and uphold their cause. I thank you in advance for the manifestation of peace, joy, and abundance because of spending time with You. These things I ask in Jesus's Holy Name. Amen.

MEDITATION EXERCISES

I like to start with a pre-determined amount of time for meditation, always with a caveat that the session could take longer. Ten minutes is always a good place to start. I've tried 5 minutes but sometimes it takes me that long to settle down and get focused.

Find your quiet place. That could be anywhere; and I mean anywhere, including a toilet stall at work. (IJS). Take a few deep cleansing breaths and start your exercises. Don't get caught up in your posture or whether your eyes should be open or closed. Do what you need to do to quiet your surroundings and settle your spirit.

Meditate with an app- This is my favorite when I'm busy & on-the go. Apps help me get in the right frame of mind to meditate. You can set reminders and alarms to ensure you spend some time with Daddy God. The two I use that are Christian based are Abide and Encounter. Encounter is free and Abide has a free and a paid version. Calm and Think Up both have free versions with Christian features you must select. Think up lets you record prayers and affirmations in your own voice. It's pretty cool.

Meditate with a project– If you love crafts, you probably do this anyway. I like to have worship music playing when I engage in a project. I find it very relaxing to color and paint. The Psalm 91 Coloring Book is awesome for this. You may enjoy puzzles, knitting, or old-fashioned whittling. It's up to you. The idea is to slow your thoughts down and bring focus on one or two ideas.

Meditate with nature– Take time to admire God's amazing creativity. Everything He has made speaks of His beauty and power, His gentleness and wisdom, His grace and love. Some relevant activities are fishing, bird watching, hiking, walking, biking in a park or on a trail, and anything else outdoorsy.

Meditate with worship- Put on some instrumental music, close your eyes and flow. Again, don't get caught up in what your body is doing. Just move as the Holy Spirit leads. As you remember the goodness of God, your movements will reflect what is in your heart. I love this! Don't be surprised if your meditation with worship goes over the time you allotted.

Meditate with the Word– I take a passage of Scripture – or a verse, and let my mind surrender to its truths. This may be during reading and meditation time, or it may carry over to thinking about that passage in the shower, while driving, or while going through my daily routine. I let my thoughts regarding that passage permeate my life. Sometimes I will meditate on a passage for days, months, or longer.

Meditate with prayer– I take my prayer needs before the Lord. Sometimes I don't even know what to say. When there are no words, I just imagine I am there before the altar of our King. In His presence is all I need. I also use my heavenly language to communicate and strengthen my focus on God.

Meditate with poetry and song writing- This may not be your thing, but it works. It embodies presence, intention, focus, and just slowing down. Try writing in patterns. The classic haiku comprises three lines, 5-7-5. But, you can definitely create your own. You could even add poems and song writing to your journal or devotional writing! Here's a sample Haiku using the characteristics of God:

> GOD is OMNIPOTENT
> HE has ALL POWER over ALL THINGS
> HE is POWER

Try your own:

_____

_____

_____

Meditate with pets- Interacting with God's creation is a wonderful way to remember that HE is the giver of life. Spending quality time with our pets remind us that we are responsible for showing care, compassion, and unconditional love. It cultivates humility and wisdom. Spend 10-15 minutes observing their behavior. Observe their loyalty. What happens when you pet them? What happens when you feed them? Their well-being depends on you.

Meditate with gardening- Grow something! Playing in the dirt can be so relaxing; a wonderful reminder that the earth is in your hands. Even with limited space, you can take part in this activity. For instance, you can grow some plants, including those used as herbs and spices indoors.

Meditate with devotional writing- One way to do this is to read the Scriptures and ask God to illuminate a word or phrase for you. Focus on that, and begin internalizing and personalizing the passage. The written Word becomes a living word addressed to you. You could even record yourself reading a verse and then listen to your recording. Sit in complete silence for a few minutes and let the Lord commune with you. Then begin writing.

Take the next 21 days to practice devotional writing.

>Day 1-7: What Does the Word Say About You?

>Day 8-14: What Does the Word Say You Have?

>Day 15-21: What Does the Word Say You Can Do?

WHAT DOES THE WORD SAY ABOUT YOU?

A Divine Pause

DAY 1

YOU ARE A PORTABLE SANCTUARY
(1 Corinth. 3:16-17), TPT

Don't you realize that together you have become God's inner sanctuary and that the Spirit of God makes his permanent home in you? Now, if someone desecrates God's inner sanctuary, God will desecrate him, for God's inner sanctuary is holy, and that is exactly who you are.

_____

_____

_____

_____

_____

_____

_____

_____

_____

_____

A Divine Pause

DAY 2

YOU ARE A CHERISHED FRIEND
(John 15:15), TPT

I have never called you 'servants,' because a master doesn't confide in his servants, and servants don't always understand what the master is doing. But I call you my most intimate and cherished friends, for I reveal to you everything that I've heard from my Father.

A Divine Pause

DAY 3

PEACE AND HOPE BELONG TO YOU
(Jeremiah 29:11), NKJV

For I know the thoughts that I think toward you, says the Lord, thoughts of peace and not of evil, to give you a future and a hope.

A Divine Pause

DAY 4

YOU ARE DESTINED FOR GOOD WORKS
(Ephesians 2:10), TPT

We have become his poetry, a re-created people that will fulfill the destiny he has given each of us, for we are joined to Jesus, the Anointed One. Even before we were born, God planned in advance our destiny and the good works we would do to fulfill it!

A Divine Pause

DAY 5

YOU ARE ONE SPIRIT WITH HIM
(1 Corinthians 6:17), TPT

But the one who joins himself to the Lord is mingled into one spirit with him.

A Divine Pause

DAY 6

YOU ARE SALT AND LIGHT.
(Matthew 5:13-16), TPT

Your lives are like salt among the people. But if you, like salt, become bland, how can your 'saltiness' be restored? Flavorless salt is good for nothing and will be thrown out and trampled on by others. Your lives light up the world. For how can you hide a city that stands on a hilltop? And who would light a lamp and then hide it in an obscure place? Instead, it's placed where everyone in the house can benefit from its light. So don't hide your light! Let it shine brightly before others, so that your commendable works will shine as light upon them, and then they will give their praise to your Father in heaven.

A Divine Pause

DAY 7

YOU ARE HEALED!
(1 Perter 2:24), TPT

He himself carried our sins in his body on the cross so that we would be dead to sin and live for righteousness. Our instant healing flowed from his wounding.

A Divine Pause

WHAT DOES THE WORD SAY YOU HAVE?

A Divine Pause

DAY 8

IT'S ALREADY DONE
(Philippians 4:19), TPT

And my God shall supply all you need according to His riches in glory by Christ Jesus.

A Divine Pause

DAY 9

GRACE GRACE GRACE
(1 Peter 4:10), TPT

Every believer has received grace gifts, so use them to serve one another as faithful stewards of the many-colored tapestry of God's grace.

A Divine Pause

DAY 10

**FORGIVENESS EVERYTIME!
(1 John 1:9), TPT**

But if we freely admit our sins when his light uncovers them, he will be faithful to forgive us every time. God is just to forgive us our sins.

A Divine Pause

DAY 11

GOD LOVES YOU PASSIONATELY AND THERE'S NOTHING YOU CAN DO ABOUT IT. (Romans 8:38-39), TPT

So now I live with the confidence that there is nothing in the universe with the power to separate us from God's love. I'm convinced that his love will triumph over death, life's troubles, fallen angels, or dark rulers in the heavens. There is nothing in our present or future circumstances that can weaken his love. There is no power above us or beneath us—no power that could ever be found in the universe that can distance us from God's passionate love, which is lavished upon us through our Lord Jesus, the Anointed One!

A Divine Pause

DAY 12

UNDENIABLE BEAUTY
(Song of Solomon 6:4), TPT

O my beloved, you are lovely. When I see you in your beauty, I see a radiant city where we will dwell as one. More pleasing than any pleasure, more delightful than any delight, you have ravished my heart, stealing away my strength to resist you. Even hosts of angels stand in awe of you.

A Divine Pause

DAY 13

SALVATION IS YOURS!
(Ephesians 1:7), TPT

Since we are now joined to Christ, we have been given the treasures of redemption by his blood—the total cancellation of our sins—all because of the cascading riches of his grace.

A Divine Pause

DAY 14

THE HOLY SPIRIT LIVE IN YOU
(1 Corinthians 6:19), TPT

Have you forgotten that your body is now the sacred temple of the Spirit of Holiness, who lives in you? You don't belong to yourself any longer, for the gift of God, the Holy Spirit, lives inside your sanctuary.

A Divine Pause

WHAT DOES THE WORD SAY YOU CAN DO?

A Divine Pause

DAY 15

**HAVE DOMINION!
(Genesis 1:28) NKJV**

Then God blessed them, and God said to them, "Be fruitful and multiply; fill the earth and subdue it; have dominion over the fish of the sea, over the birds of the air, and over every living thing that moves on the earth."

A Divine Pause

DAY 16

MOVE FROM A POSTURE OF VICTORY!
(Luke 10:19) TPT

Now you understand that I have imparted to you my authority to trample over his kingdom. You will trample upon every demon before you and overcome every power satan possesses. Absolutely nothing will harm you as you walk in this authority.

A Divine Pause

DAY 17

**RELEASE IT!
(1 Peter 5:7), TPT**

Pour out all your worries and stress upon him and leave them there, for he always tenderly cares for you.

A Divine Pause

DAY 18

ASK BOLDLY. BELIEVE COURAGEOUSLY. (Mark 11:24), TPT

This is the reason I urge you to boldly believe for whatever you ask for in prayer—be convinced that you have received it and it will be yours.

A Divine Pause

DAY 19

YOU CAN DO IT; WITH THE RIGHT PARTNER. (Philippians 4:12-13), TPT

I know what it means to lack, and I know what it means to experience overwhelming abundance. For I'm trained in the secret of overcoming all things, whether in fullness or in hunger. And I find that the strength of Christ's explosive power infuses me to conquer every difficulty.

A Divine Pause

DAY 20

EVEN GREATER MIRACLES ARE IN YOUR HANDS.
(John 14:12), TPT

I tell you this timeless truth: The person who follows me in faith, believing in me, will do the same mighty miracles that I do—even greater miracles than these because I go to be with my Father!

A Divine Pause

DAY 21

ACCESS GRANTED! GO FOR IT!
(Ezra 10:4), TPT

Rise up; this matter is in your hands. We will support you, so take courage and do it.

A Divine Pause

CONCLUSION

COVID-19 was the initial DIVINE PAUSE in my life that caused me to slow down and find a lump in my breast. During this DIVINE PAUSE I learned to meditate and to connect with God on another level. During this DIVINE PAUSE, I also learned the meaning of resiliency and gained a new appreciation for life and, living life more abundantly. In addition, during this DIVINE PAUSE I learned that I was not quite ready to retire. I have more service in me for this country and, moreover for the Kingdom of God. The DIVINE PAUSE helps me to show up whole in every situation. Slow down and get instruction for your destiny.

Meditation is biblical. As is the case for all good things, there are counterfeit versions. Meditation should not be spooky or weird. When coupled with Scripture and a focus on the Father, it's very rewarding. There are endless spiritual, mental, and physical benefits when it is incorporated in one's lifestyle. It's part of my wellness routine. It's how I take care of me. You'll be amazed at how you soar through life's hills and valleys with faith and a Kingdom perspective.

Finally, the doctor's report matches the report I received from Holy Spirit earlier this year. This is what the letter said, " Mrs. Clarkriley, we wish to inform you that your recent ultrasound on 05/05/2021 shows no sign of breast cancer". I am healed! I thank GOD for walking with me through this; for connecting with me during our time and covering me with HIS peace.

Meditation is my path to HIS PRESENCE. I hope you add it to your toolbelt. My final "ah ha" moment is the realization that writing a book is meditation! Thank you Lord!

MEDITATION RESOURCES

APPS:
Abide, Encounter, Whispers from God, Pray, Calm, Think Up

A Divine Pause

REFERENCES AND CITED WORKS

Definitions-Oxford Languages. Oxford University Press. www.google.com, 2021

www.mindworks.org

Focus on the Family, Mindfulness: A Christian Approach, September 2019

Richard J. Foster. Celebration of Discipline. 1992

James W. Goll, Godencounters.com

Vivien Hibbert. Worship, Prayer, and Meditation. April 2021

April Motl. What Does Meditation Mean in the Bible?. www.christianity.com, June 2019

Chad Napier. Can a Christian Practice Buddhist Meditation Methods?. www.christianity.com, June 2019

Madeline Pena. Christian Disciplines. Christian Meditation: Definition, Biblical Examples and More, https://justdisciple.com/christian-meditation/

Dr. Robert Puff. Psychology Today. Meditation for Modern Life, July 2013

Gary Thomas. Sacred Pathways. Zondervan, October 2010

Craig von Busek. What is Soaking Prayer. https://www1.cbn.com/question/what-is-soaking-prayer